Where Kindness Leads The Little Mouse Home

Written by

Dan Jarvis

First Published in 2025 by Blossom Spring Publishing
Where Kindness Leads The Little Mouse Home Copyright © 2025 Dan Jarvis
ISBN 978-1-917938-25-9
E: admin@blossomspringpublishing.com
W: www.blossomspringpublishing.com
Dan Jarvis as the author and as the illustrator,
has been asserted in accordance with the Copyright, Designs and Patents Act,1988.
All rights reserved under International Copyright Law.
Contents and/or cover may not be reproduced in whole or in part without the express written consent of the publisher.

There once was a tiny, but brave little Mouse,
who had set off exploring a long way from his house.

He had to get home before it got late,
but his sense of direction was really not great.

He stumbled across a mighty long river,

"I don't remember this," he thought, as he started to quiver.

Out of the water, a duck reared his head

"I can help you across if you like," he said.

"Oh, thank you," said the mouse, and he climbed on his back.

"All aboard," said the duck. "Quack! Quack! Quack!"

As they crossed the river and reached the other side, the mouse said, "thank you for the ride."

"You're welcome," said the duck, "but that's as far as I go. Do you know the way now?"

The mouse replied, "I think so."

Off ran the mouse as he went on his way,

"I have to get home before the end of the day."

Next in his way were Mountains that reached the sky,

"I definitely can't climb that, it's far too high."

Out popped a bird.
"Need a lift?" he said,

"Oh, yes, please kind bird, I need to get home to my bed."

The mouse grabbed on tightly as the bird soared so high, over the mountains and the clouds in the sky.

They landed on the other side, "thank you," said the mouse, feeling like he was one step closer to his house.

"You're welcome," said the bird, "but that's as far as I go. Do you know the way now?"

The mouse muttered back, "I think so."

Onto the monkey's back he held on so tight,

"Are you ready?" said the monkey, as he climbed a tree and took flight.

Swinging this way and that way from tree to tree!

And just like that, from the snakes they were free.

"Oh, thank you, kind monkey,
for saving me there,
it's really nice to meet animals
that care."

"You're welcome," said the monkey,
"but that's as far as I go.
Do you know the way now?"

The mouse mumbled,
"I think so."

The sun in the sky was beginning to fall,
there wasn't long left before it was darkness for all.

The mouse started to worry that he
would never get home.
And he'd be stranded in the dark
and all on his own.

Out popped a Cheetah as happy as can be,
"I can run really fast, want to ride with me?"

"Oh, yes, please, kind cheetah,
are you really that quick?"

"Jump on," he said. "I'll have you home in a tick."

Off set the cheetah, he was rapid, he went far,
the mouse felt like he was driving a super-fast racing car!

As the mouse opened his eyes, in the distance
he saw, his mum standing right outside his front door.

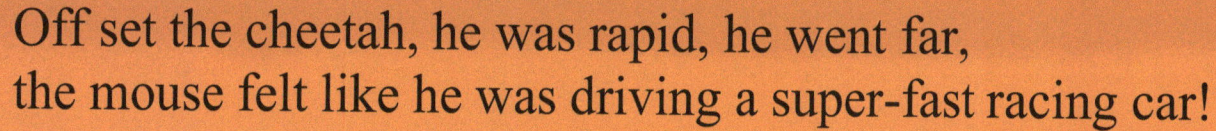

"Thank you, kind cheetah, for getting me here
and saving me from the dark, my biggest fear."

"You're welcome," he said,
"but that's as far as I go.
Do you know the way now?"

The mouse cheered, "Oh, I think so!!"

As the mouse skipped home to give his mummy a squeeze, he looked back at his journey and through all of the trees.

To the cheetah, the monkey, the bird and the duck, he really couldn't believe his luck.

All of them helped him and really didn't mind

They did what we all should do and were nothing but kind.

Go back and read again.
Can you spot any differences in the animals?

About the Author

Dan lives in Kent with his Wife and two boys.

He has a keen interest in football and a real passion for music. Currently, he plays guitar in a band that performs regularly at pubs throughout Kent and the South-East.

His passion for writing Children's books came from his two young boys, constantly reading bedtime stories and getting inspiration and ideas from George and Harry.

He hopes to turn many more ideas from his children into fun and educational stories that many families can enjoy together.

www.blossomspringpublishing.com

www.ingramcontent.com/pod-product-compliance
Lightning Source LLC
Chambersburg PA
CBHW040031050426
42453CB00002B/81